G000252605

HINTS ON
ETIQUETTE

AND THE USAGES OF SOCIETY

WITH A GLANCE AT BAD HABITS

By Your Guide

HINTS ON ETIQUETTE

Hints on Etiquette, etc., was first published in 1834 by Messrs. Longman, Rees, Orme, Brown, Green, and Longman.

This edition published in 2005 by Summersdale Publishers Ltd.

Condition of Sale

Summersdale Publishers Ltd
46 West Street
Chichester
West Sussex
PO19 1RP
UK

www.summersdale.com

Printed and bound in Great Britain

ISBN 1 84024 456 9

Editor's Note

Originally published in 1856, this guide on how to behave in a polite and appropriate way in various social situations still has valuable lessons for the contemporary reader. Nobody likes to be considered 'improper', 'vulgar' or 'obtuse', nor the kind of person who doesn't know when it is acceptable to offer a lady a glass of wine. This Victorian handbook contains instructions on such themes as introductions ('Should you, whilst walking with your friend, meet an acquaintance, never introduce them') and dinner parties ('Eat peas with a dessert spoon; and curry also').

Indispensable reading for those wanting to act with a certain dignity in society (especially those in the country 'where the tone of society is altogether lower'), it is also a delightful diversion for the rest of us who are thankful that life is no longer so complicated.

Introduction

This is not written for those *who do* but for those who do *not know what is proper*, comprising a large portion of highly respectable and estimable people, who have had no opportunity of becoming acquainted with the usages of the (so termed) 'best society'; therefore, do not let the 'select' sneer, and say – 'Oh, everybody knows *that*; there is nothing *new* here'. Even *they* may be mistaken, and many may profit who will not choose to *own* how much they are indebted to this little book.

It would be absurd to suppose, those persons who constitute the upper ranks of the middle classes in London are ignorant of the regulations here laid down; but in the country (especially in the mercantile districts), where the tone of society is altogether lower, it is far otherwise, although country people may not feel inclined to *acknowledge* what is, nevertheless, strictly true.

If these ' hints' save the blush but upon *one cheek*, or smooth the path into 'society' of only *one* honest family, the object of the author will be attained.

London, 20 Jan. 1836

Contents

Hints on Etiquette
&c., &c.

Etiquette is the barrier which society draws around itself as a protection against offences the 'law' cannot touch – a shield against the intrusion of the impertinent, the improper, and the vulgar

a guard against those obtuse persons

– a guard against those obtuse persons who, having neither talent nor delicacy, would be continually thrusting themselves into the society of men to whom their presence might (from the difference of feeling and habit) be offensive, and even insupportable.

Many unthinking persons consider the observance of Etiquette to be nonsensical and unfriendly, as consisting of unmeaning forms, practised only by the *silly* and the idle; an opinion which arises from their not having reflected on the *reasons* that have caused certain rules to be established, indispensable to the well-being of society, and without which, indeed, it would inevitably fall to pieces, and be destroyed.

Much misconstruction and unpleasant feeling arises, especially in country towns, from not knowing what is *'expected'*, or necessary to be done on certain occasions, resulting sometimes from the prevalence of local customs, with which the world in general are not supposed to be acquainted.

Besides, in a mercantile country like England, people are continually rising in the world.

Shopkeepers become merchants, and mechanics manufacturers; with the possession of wealth they acquire a taste for the luxuries of life, expensive furniture, and gorgeous plate; also numberless superfluities, with the use of which they are only imperfectly acquainted. But although their capacities for enjoyment increase, it rarely occurs that the polish of their manners keeps pace with the rapidity of their advancement: such persons are often painfully reminded that wealth alone is insufficient to protect them from the mortifications a limited acquaintance with society will entail upon the ambitious. Pride often deters people from seeking the advice of the experienced, when the opportunity of receiving it is presented. It is to be hoped that the following remarks will furnish a guide through the intricacies of conventional usage, without risk to the sensitive, or the humiliation of *publicly* proclaiming the deficiencies of an imperfect education.

In all cases, the observances of the Metropolis (as the seat of refinement) should be received as the standard of good breeding.

Introductions

Never 'introduce' people to each other, without a previous understanding that it will be agreeable to both.

There are many reasons why people ought never to be introduced to the acquaintance of each other, without the consent of each party previously obtained. A man may suit the taste, and be agreeable enough  **reasons why people ought never to be introduced** to *one*, without being equally so to the *rest* of his friends – nay, as it often happens, decidedly unpleasing; a stupid person may be delighted with the society of a man of learning or talent, to whom in return such an acquaintance may prove an annoyance and a clog, as one incapable of offering an interchange of thought, or an idea worth listening to.

But if you should find an agreeable person in private society, who seems desirous of making your acquaintance, there cannot be an objection to your meeting his advances half way, although the ceremony of an 'introduction' may not have taken place; his presence in your friend's house being a sufficient guarantee for his respectability, as of course if he were an improper person he would not be there.

Should you, whilst walking with your friend, meet an acquaintance, never introduce them.

In making 'introductions', take care to present the person of the lower rank to him of the higher; that is, the commoner should be presented to the peer, not the peer to the commoner; Dr. A. to Lord B., not Lord B. to Dr. A. Observe the same rule with ladies – the lady (as a female) claiming the highest rank, it is to *her* the gentleman must be presented, not the lady to the gentleman.

Be cautious how you take an intimate friend *uninvited* even to the house of those with whom you may be equally intimate, as there is always a feeling of jealousy that another should share your thoughts and feelings to the same extent as themselves, although good breeding will induce them to behave *civilly* to your friend on your account.

Friendship springs up from sources so subtle and undefinable, that it cannot be *forced* into particular channels; and whenever the attempt has been made, it has usually been unsuccessful.

Never make acquaintances in coffee-houses or other public places. As no person who respects himself does so, you may reasonably suspect any advances made to *you*.

An adherence to Etiquette is a mark of respect; if a man be *worth knowing*, he is surely worth the trouble to approach properly. It will likewise relieve you from the awkwardness of being acquainted with people of whom you might at times be ashamed, or be obliged under many circumstances to '*cut*'.

A neglect of, or an adherence to, the forms of society, in others towards yourself, is oftentimes the only way in which you are enabled to judge if your acquaintance be *really* **you would run a risk of being mortified** considered desirable. You will meet with professions of civility and friendship in the world as mere matters of course; and were you to act upon what people *say*, instead of what they *do*, you would run a risk of being mortified, which no person of proper pride would choose to encounter; especially if the other party *be*, or *assume to be*, of higher rank than yourself: we never knew a person, really desirous of forming a friendship with another, neglect, either by word or deed, the means of accomplishing such an object.

It is, however, understood in society, that a person having been *properly* introduced to you, has some claim on your good offices in future; you cannot therefore slight him without good reason, and the chance of being called to an account for it.

Letters of Introduction

If you have letters of introduction from one friend to another, do *not take them*, but *send them*, with your card of address. If he be a *gentleman*, he will return your visits as soon as possible; at any rate it will give him an option, which by taking your letters in person you *do not do*, but rather force yourself upon him whether *he will or not*. If your letters be on business only, no ceremony is necessary – take them at once. In all such matters never trust to a *second* that which may be so much better done by yourself.

There cannot be a more awkward situation for both parties than whilst one is reading a letter with the endeavour to discover who the other can be, or a position in which the bearer looks so foolish, or feels so uncomfortable – then comes the bow, a cold shake of the hand, with the few civil words of course – and all because you come upon a stranger who is unprepared; therefore give him time to read the letter you bring, and to consider how he may best show his regard for your introducer by his attentions to yourself.

If a gentleman be the bearer of an 'introduction' to *you*, leave a card with him without fail, if it

give him time to read the letter you bring

be only as an acknowledgement of having received your friend's letter; there is no rudeness so great as to leave it unnoticed – it is a slight to the stranger as well as to the introducer, which no subsequent attentions will cancel: you are not obliged to *invite* him, as *that* is a matter of choice.

For the same reasons, a letter should never remain unanswered a moment longer than is absolutely unavoidable. Should you not have time to answer it *fully*, an acknowledgement merely is better than no notice taken of it at all.

An adherence to these rules will prevent your exposure to any coldness or flight you might otherwise incur.

Do not imagine these little ceremonies to be insignificant and beneath your attention: they are the customs of society; and if you do not conform to them, you will gain the unenviable distinction of being pointed out as an ignorant, ill-bred person. Not that you may *care* the more for strangers by showing them civility, but you should scrupulously avoid the imputation of being deficient in good breeding; and if you do not choose to be polite for *their* sakes, you ought to be so for *your own*.

Marriage

When a man marries, it is understood that all former acquaintanceship *ends*, unless he intimate a desire to renew it, by sending you his own and his wife's card, if near, or by letter, if distant. If this be neglected, be sure no further intercourse is desired.

In the first place – a bachelor is seldom *very particular* in the choice of his companions. So long as he is amused, he will associate freely enough with those whose morals and habits would point them out as highly dangerous persons to introduce into the sanctity of domestic life.

Secondly – a married man has the tastes of *another* to consult; and the friend of the *husband* may not be equally acceptable to the *wife*.

Besides – newly-married people may wish to limit the circle of their friends, from

a married man has the tastes of *another* to consult

praiseworthy motives of economy. When a man first '*sets up*' in the world, the burden of an extensive and indiscriminate acquaintance may be felt in various ways.

Many have had cause to regret the weakness of mind which allowed them to plunge into a vortex of gaiety and expense they could ill afford, from which they have found it difficult to extricate themselves, and the effects of which have proved a serious evil to them in after-life.

Dinners

Of the etiquette of a dinner party, it is extremely difficult to say any thing, because fashions are continually changing, even at the best tables; and what is considered the height of good taste one year, is declared vulgar the next; besides which, certain houses and *sets* have certain customs, peculiar to that clique, and all who do not conform *exactly* to their methods are looked upon as vulgar persons, ignorant of good breeding. This is a mistake commonly fallen into by the little 'great' in the country, where the circle constituting '*society*' is necessarily so small, that its members cannot fail to acquire the same habits, feelings, and observances. However, a few hints may not be thrown away, always recollecting people can only become ridiculous by attempting to be too *fine*. I am, of course, supposing my readers to be acquainted with the *decencies* of life.

* To avoid misconstruction, it will be as well to define what is *meant* by the term 'little great', beginning by showing what is *not*. It is NOT that numerous class (however respectable), professional and mercantile, found in and about every country town; those merely *great little*, who, without any other qualification than the possession of a few thousand pounds, constitute themselves the aristocracy of the place: but a very different body – namely, the *old*, solid, 'COUNTY PEOPLE', the descendants of patrician families, the Squirearchy, with incomes of from seven to ten thousands a year, and the customary representatives in parliament (until lately)

of their town or county – persons who are of great *local influence* and importance, on account of their descent and wealth, but who, notwithstanding, become insignificant and merely *units in the mass*, amidst the brilliant statesmen, the talent, the splendour of rank and fashion which adorn and elevate the metropolis.

When the members of the party have all assembled in the drawing-room, the master or mistress of the house will point out which lady you are to take into the dining-room, according to some real or fancied standard of precedence, rank (if there be rank), age, or general importance; that is, the married before the single, etc., etc.; or they will show their tact, by making those companions,

who are most likely to be agreeable to each other. Give the lady the wall coming down stairs, take her into the room, and seat yourself by her side.

If you pass to dine merely from one room to another, offer your right arm to the lady.

* Remember that it is the *lady* who at all times takes precedence, not the gentleman. A person led a princess out of the room before her husband (who was doing the same to a lady of lower rank); in his over-politeness, he said, 'Pardonnez que nous vous précédons', quite forgetting that it was the *princess* and not *he* who led the way.

Well-bred people arrive as nearly at the appointed dinner hour as they can. It is a very vulgar assumption of importance purposely to arrive half an hour **vulgar assumption of importance** behind time; besides the folly of allowing eight or ten hungry people such a tempting opportunity of discussing your foibles.

* Of those passages marked with an asterisk, the groundwork has been taken from the MS. note-book of a lady of rank.

The lady of the house will of course take the head of the table, and the gentleman of the highest rank will sit at her *right* hand; the gentleman next in rank will be placed on the left of the hostess, so that she may be supported by the two persons of the most consideration (who will assist her to carve).

It is the custom at present for the lady of the house to be the *last*, and to *follow* her guests into the dining-room.

The gentleman of the house takes the bottom of the table, and on each side of *him* must be placed *the two ladies highest in rank*. You will find a party of *ten* convenient, as it admits of an equal distribution of the sexes: neither two men nor two women like to sit together.

It is considered vulgar to take fish or soup twice.

The *reason* for not being helped twice to fish or soup at a large dinner party is – because by doing so you keep three parts of the company staring at you whilst waiting for the second course, which is spoiling, much to the annoyance of the mistress of the house. The selfish greediness, therefore, of so doing constitutes its vulgarity.

At a family dinner it is of less importance, and is consequently often done.

Do not ask any lady to take wine, until you see she has *finished* her fish or soup.

This exceedingly absurd and troublesome custom is very properly giving way at the best tables to the more reasonable one of the gentleman helping the lady to wine next to whom he may be seated, or a servant will hand it round.

But if either a lady or a gentleman be invited to take wine at table, they must *never refuse*; it is very *gauche* so to do. They need not drink half a glass with each person, but merely taste of it.

At every respectable table you will find *silver* forks; being broader, they are in all respects more convenient than steel for fish or vegetables.

At family dinners, where the common household bread is used, it should never be cut less than an inch and a half thick. There is nothing more plebian than *thin* bread at dinner.

There is nothing more plebian than *thin* bread

NEVER *use your knife to convey* your food to your mouth, *under any circumstances*; it is unnecessary, and glaringly vulgar. Feed yourself with a *fork* or *spoon*, *nothing else* – a knife is only to be used for cutting.

If at dinner you are requested to help any one to sauce, do not pour it over the meat or vegetables, but on one side. If you should have to carve and help a joint, do not load a person's plate – it is vulgar: also in serving soup, one ladleful to each plate is sufficient.

Fish does not require a knife, but should be divided by the aid of a piece of bread.

The application of a knife to fish is likely to destroy the delicacy of its flavour; besides which, fish sauces are often acidulated; acids corrode steel, and draw from it a disagreeable taste. In the North, where lemon or vinegar is very generally used for salmon and many other kinds of fish, the objection becomes more apparent.

Eat PEAS with a dessert spoon; and curry also.

Tarts and puddings are to be eaten with a *spoon*.

As a general rule – in helping any one at table, never use a knife where you can use a spoon.

Making a noise in chewing or breathing hard in eating, are both unseemly habits, and ought to be eschewed.

Many people make a disgusting noise with their lips, by inhaling their breath strongly

whilst taking soup – a habit which should be carefully avoided.

* You cannot use your knife, or fork, or teeth too quietly.

Do not *press* people to eat more than they appear to like, nor *insist* upon their tasting of any particular dish: you may so far recommend one, as to mention that it is considered 'excellent'. Remember that tastes differ, and viands, which please *you*, may be objects of dislike to *others*; and that in consequence of your urgency, very young or very modest people may feel themselves compelled to partake of what may be most disagreeable to them.

* Do not pick your teeth *much* at table, as, however satisfactory a practice to yourself, to witness it is not a pleasant thing.

Ladies should never dine with their gloves on – unless their hands are not fit to be seen.

Servants should wait at table in *clean white gloves*: there are few things more disagreeable than the thumb of a clumsy waiter in your plate.

Finger glasses, filled with *warm* water, come on with the **the *filthy* custom of gargling** dessert. Wet a corner of your napkin, and wipe your mouth, then rinse your fingers; but do not practise the *filthy* custom of gargling your mouth at table, albeit the usage prevails amongst a few, who think, *because* it is a foreign habit, it cannot be disgusting.

* Never pare an apple or a pear for a lady unless she desire you, and then be careful to use your fork to hold it: you may sometimes offer to *divide a very large pear* with a person, or for them.

At some of the best houses, coffee is brought into the dining-room before the gentlemen quit the table – a very good custom, as it *gently* prevents excess, the guests retiring to the ladies immediately afterwards; it also allows those who have other engagements to take coffee before they quit the house. Coffee should be brought in at an hour previously appointed, *without the bell being rung for it*, but a sufficient interval must be allowed, lest the host seem chary of his wine. For instance, nine o'clock is a good hour, if the dinner were at six; or ten o'clock for one which commenced at seven.

Never order other people's servants about

Do not suppose that it will exalt you in the opinion of others, by speaking harshly and imperatively to servants, or add at all to your consequence. Never order other people's servants about. At a strange table, say 'if you please', and 'thank you': it may be said in a manner that will not encourage familiarity.

Nothing indicates a well-bred man more than a proper mode of eating his dinner. A man may pass muster by *dressing well*, and may sustain himself tolerably in conversation; but if he be not perfectly 'au fait', *dinner* will betray him

It is a piece of superlative folly for men who dine at a house to take their round hats into the drawing-room: it answers no purpose at all; and the necessity of giving them to a servant on entering the dinner room, creates confusion.

Invitations to dine should be answered to the lady. Invitations to a ball should be in the lady's name, and the answer of course sent to her.

It is customary, when you have been out dining, to leave a card upon the lady the next day, or as soon after as may be convenient. Attentions of this sort are not to be expected from professional men, as Doctors, Lawyers, etc., *their* time being too valuable to sacrifice in making visits of mere ceremony; therefore, do not attribute such omission to any want of respect, but to its proper cause – *time more usefully occupied.*

When a man is about to be married, he usually gives a dinner to his bachelor friends; which is understood to be their congé, unless he choose to renew their acquaintance.

Smoking

If you are so unfortunate as to have contracted the low habit of smoking, be careful to practise it under certain restrictions; at least, so long as you are desirous of being centered fit for civilised society.

The first mark of a gentleman is a sensitive regard for the feelings of others; therefore, smoke where it is least likely to prove personally offensive by making your clothes smell; then **breath smelling of onions** wash your mouth, and brush your teeth. What man of delicacy could presume to address a lady with his breath smelling of onions?

Yet tobacco is equally odious. The tobacco smoker, in *public*, is the most selfish animal imaginable; he perseveres in contaminating the pure and fragrant air, careless whom he annoys, and is but the fitting inmate of a tavern.

Smoking in the streets, or in a theatre, is only practised by shop-boys, pseudo-fashionables – and the 'SWELL MOB'.

All songs that you may see written in praise of smoking in magazines or newspapers, or hear sung upon the stage, are *puffs*, paid for by the proprietors of cigar divans and tobacco shops, to make their trade popular – therefore, never believe nor be deluded by them.

Never be seen in cigar divans

Never be seen in cigar divans or billiard rooms; they are frequented, at best, by an equivocal set. *No good* can be gained there – and a man loses his respectability by being seen entering or coming out of such places.

Never sit in the boxes of a theatre with your *hat on*; it is an insult to the rest of the audience, especially if there be ladies.

On entering a coffee-house, and sitting down, *take off your hat*; it is only a proper mark of respect to your own class, towards whom you should *pay* the same deference you *exact* from others.

Snuff

As snuff-taking is merely an idle, dirty habit, practised by stupid people in the unavailing endeavour to clear their stolid intellect, and is not a custom particularly offensive to their neighbours, it may be left to each individual taste as to whether it be continued or not. An 'Elégant' cannot take *much* snuff without decidedly 'losing caste'.

'Doctor', said an old gentleman, who was an inveterate snuff-taker, to a physician, 'is it true that snuff destroys the olfactory nerves, clogs, and otherwise injures the brain?' 'It cannot be true', was the caustic reply, 'since *those who have any brains never take snuff at all.*'

Fashion

But few things betray greater imbecility of mind than a servile imitation of the extravagancies of any fashionable monster. A man possessed of the delicate and proper feelings of a gentleman would deem himself *degraded* by copying another, even to the curling of a whisker, or the tie of a cravat; as, by so doing, he could only show the world of how little importance he felt himself, and the very poor opinion he entertained of his own taste.

Fashion and *gentility* are very distinct things – for which reason, people,

Fashion and gentility are very distinct things

really of the highest rank, are too proud to become *martyrs* to any prevailing mode; and the man of true taste will limit his compliance with the caprices of fashion to the not appearing *equally conspicuous* for its utter neglect.

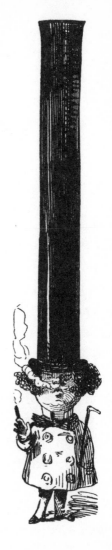

Dress

It is in bad taste to dress in the extreme of fashion; and, in general, those only do so who have no other claim to distinction – leave it, in these, times, to shopmen and pickpockets. There are certain occasions, however, when you may dress as gaily as you please, observing the maxim of the ancient poet, to be 'great on great occasions'. Men often think when they wear a fashionably cut coat, an embroidered waistcoat, with a profusion of chains and other trinkets, that they are well dressed, entirely overlooking the less obtrusive, but more certain, marks of a refined taste. The grand points are – well-made shoes, clean gloves, a white pocket handkerchief, and, *above all*, an easy and graceful deportment.

Do not affect singularity in dress, by wearing out-of-the-way hats or gaudy

waistcoats, etc., and so become contemptibly conspicuous; nothing is more easy than to attract attention in such a manner, since it requires neither sense nor taste. A shrewd old gentleman said of one of these 'ninnies', that *'he would rather be taken for a* FOOL, *than not be noticed at all'*.

Never affect the 'ruffianly' style of dress, unless, indeed, you hold a brilliant position in society. A nobleman, or an exceedingly elegant and refined man, will occasionally disguise himself, and assume the 'ruffian', as it **your *dress* is as *coarse* as your *mind*** amuses him to mark the surprise of people at the *contrast* between his *appearance* and his *manners*; but if *you* have no such pretensions, let your costume be as unostentatious as possible, lest people only remark that 'your *dress* is as *coarse* as your *mind'*.

Always wear your gloves in church or in a theatre.

Avoid wearing jewellery, unless it be in very good taste, and then only at proper seasons. This is the age of mosaic gold and other trash; and by dint of swindling, any one *may* become ' flashy' at a small expense: recollect that every shop-boy can coarsely imitate your 'outward and visible sign' if he choose to save his money for that purpose. If you *will* stand out in 'high and bold relief', endeavour to become eminent for some virtue or talent, that people may say, 'There goes the *celebrated* (not the notorious) Mr. So-and-so'.

It is a delicate subject to hint at the incongruities of a lady's dress – yet, alas! it forces itself upon our notice when we see a female attired with elaborate gorgeousness, picking her way along the sloppy streets, after a week's snow and a three days' thaw, *walking* in a dress only fit for a carriage. When country people visit London, and see a lady enveloped in ermine and velvets, reclining in a carriage, they are apt to imagine it is the fashionable dress, and adopt it accordingly, overlooking the coronet emblazoned on the panels, and that its occupant is a duchess or a marchioness at the least, and that were the same person to *walk*, she would be in a very different costume, and then only attended by a footman.

Music

It is the misfortune of musical people generally to be such enthusiasts, that, once beginning, they seldom know when to leave off: there are few things a greater *seccatura* than a long 'Concerto', or duett upon

The listeners get fidgetty and tired

the pianoforte, or an 'Air with (endless) variations'. The listeners get fidgetty and tired, although they are usually too polite to say so. I once sat next to a foreigner, who had endured with exemplary patience a tedious 'Concerto', and who, when it was finished, applauded vehemently, then, turning round to me with a droll expression of countenance, said, *'perchè si finisce'.* *

* 'Because it's finished.'

A song *now* and *then* is very desirable, as it is a relief to conversation, but half a dozen consecutively, even from St. Cecilia in person, would become a bore; besides which, people are now accustomed to hear popular songs executed by those whose profession it is, with a superiority rarely attainable in private life, so that amateurs seldom do more than provoke unfortunate comparisons. However, when highly-gifted musicians *are* found in private society, we have generally observed their *delicacy* to be in proportion to their *excellence.*

But the case is much worse when a professional 'violinist' is admitted into a private party: he either flourishes away, unconscious that he is not in an orchestra, or else, desirous to prove his superiority over the *'dillettanti'*, he overpowers them with a tone that might fill a cathedral. The best fiddles *scream* too much in (comparatively) small rooms, however delicately they may be played; besides that few even of the first English musicians seem to understand what an *'accompaniment'* really means, each performer being too intent on making his particular instrument heard above the rest, to care about the *subject*, or to feel that an 'accompaniment' should be subdued, and *subservient* to the voice.

We once heard the silver tones of an exquisite singer completely destroyed, between the shriekings of a fiddle, the vain-glorious grumblings of a violoncello, and the wheezings of a dyspeptic flute.

Dancing

With the etiquette of a ballroom, so far as it goes, there are but few people unacquainted. Certain persons are appointed to act as stewards, or there will be a 'master of the ceremonies', whose office it is to see that every thing be conducted in a proper manner: if you are entirely a stranger, it is to *them* you must apply for a partner, and point out (quietly) any young lady with whom you should like to dance, when, if there be no obvious inequality of rank, they will present you for that purpose; should there be an objection,

she will unhesitatingly 'decline the honour'

they will probably select some one they consider more suitable; but do not, on any account, go to a strange lady by yourself, and request her to dance, as she will unhesitatingly 'decline the honour', and think you an impertinent fellow for your presumption.

Any presentation to a lady in a public ballroom, for the mere purpose of dancing, does not entitle you to claim her acquaintance afterwards; therefore, should you meet her the next day, do not attempt to address her. At most, you may lift your hat; but even that is better avoided – unless, indeed, she first bow – as neither she nor her friends can know *who* or *what* you are.

Do not wear *black* or coloured gloves, lest your partner look sulky; even should you be in *mourning*, wear *white* gloves, *not black*. People in DEEP *mourning* have no business in a ballroom at all.

LEAD the lady through the quadrille; do not *drag* her, nor clasp her hand as if it were made of wood, lest she not unjustly think you a boor.

You will not, if you are wise, stand up in a quadrille without knowing something of the figure; and if you are master of a few of the steps, *so much the better*. But dance quietly, do not kick and caper about, nor sway your body to and fro: dance only *from the hips downwards*; and lead the lady as lightly as you would tread a measure with a spirit of gossamer.

Do not pride yourself on doing 'steps neatly', unless you are ambitious of being taken for a dancing-master; between whom and to dance like a *gentleman* there is a great difference.

If a lady should civilly decline to dance with you, making an excuse, and you chance to see her dancing afterwards, do not take any notice of it, nor be offended with her.

there are many bursting hearts within white satin dresses

It might *not* be that she *despised you*, but that she *preferred another*. We cannot always fathom the hidden springs which influence a woman's actions, and there are many bursting hearts within white satin dresses; therefore do not insist upon the fulfilment of established regulations 'de rigueur'. Besides, it is a hard case that women should be compelled to dance with everybody offered them, at the alternative of not being allowed to enjoy themselves at all.

If a friend be engaged when you request her to dance, and she promises to be your partner for the next or any of the following dances, do not neglect her when the time comes, but be in readiness to fulfil your office as her cavalier, or she may think that you have studiously slighted her, besides preventing her obliging some one else. Even inattention and forgetfulness, by showing, how little you care for a lady, form in themselves a tacit insult.

Above all, do not be prone to quarrel in a ballroom; it disturbs the harmony of the company, and should be avoided, if possible. Recollect that a thousand little **do not be prone to quarrel in a ballroom** derelictions from strict propriety may occur through the *ignorance* or *stupidity* of the aggressor, and not from any intention to annoy: remember also, that *really well-bred* women will not thank you for making them conspicuous by over-officiousness in their defence, unless, indeed, there be any serious or glaring violation of decorum. In small matters, ladies are both able and willing to take care of themselves, and would prefer being allowed to overwhelm the unlucky offender in their own way.

Of Society in General

If you meet a lady of your acquaintance in the street, it is *her part* to notice *you first*,

she may not choose to acknowledge you

unless, indeed, you are very intimate. The reason is, if *you* bow to a lady first, she may not choose to acknowledge you, and there is no remedy; but if *she* bow to *you* – you, *as a gentleman, cannot cut her.*

Never *nod* to a lady in the street, neither be satisfied with touching your hat, *but take it off* – it is a courtesy her sex demands.

* Do not insist upon pulling off your glove on a very hot day when you shake hands with a lady. If it *be off*, why, all very well; but it is better to run the risk of being considered ungallant, than to present a *clammy* ungloved hand.

If you meet a friend in the street – in a coffee-house, shop, or indeed *any* public place, never address him by name, at least, not so loudly as that others may hear it: sensitive people do not like to be 'shown up' to strangers as 'Mr. Jones', or 'Mr. Smith', and so attract disagreeable notice. Accost your friend *quietly*; and do not *roar out* 'Ah! Mr. Smith! how do you do, Mr. Smith': it is very offensive, and shows a great want of proper delicacy.

Do not *strain* after great people – for, although they like the homage, inasmuch as it flatters their vanity, yet they despise the dispenser of it. Pay them, however, all proper respect; but do not forget what is due to yourself.

As a general rule – it is the place of the superior in rank to speak first to the inferior.

an opportunity of behaving superciliously If you have been in society with a nobleman, and should chance to meet him again elsewhere, leave it to him to speak first, or to recognise you. If *you* claim *his* acquaintance, you give him an opportunity of behaving superciliously to you, which would be as well avoided.

An unfortunate Clerk of the Treasury, who, because he was in the receipt of a good salary, and being also a ' triton amongst the minnows' of Clapham Common, fancied himself a great man, dined at the B—f S—k Club, where he sat next to a noble Duke, who, desirous of putting him at ease with himself, conversed freely with him, yet probably forgot even the existence of such a person half an hour afterwards. Meeting his Grace in the street some days after, and encouraged by his previous condescension, the hero of the quill, bent on claiming his acquaintance, accosted him in a familiar 'hail fellow-well-met-ish' manner – 'Ah, my Lord, how d'ye do?' The Duke looked surprised. 'May I know, Sir, to *whom* I have the honour of speaking?' said his Grace, drawing up. 'Oh! why – don't you know? We dined together at the B—f S—k Club, the other evening! – I'm MR. TIMMS OF THE TREASURY!!' 'Then', said the Duke, turning on his heel, 'MR. TIMMS OF THE TREASURY, I wish you a *good morning*'.

We hear much of the courtesy, urbanity, and condescension of the aristocracy, and those who, in all humility, bow down, will experience it; but woe to the unfortunate wight, *who respects himself*, who dares to assert his own opinions in contradiction to theirs! For an *inferior* in rank to be *superior* in intellect abases them, and they *will dislike him* for it accordingly.

Advice to Tradespeople

By tradespeople I do not mean merchants or manufacturers, but shopkeepers and retailers of various goods, who will do well to remember that people are respectable in their own sphere only, and that when  they attempt to step out of it *they cease to be so*. When exceptions are made by the world, it is generally in favour of brilliant genius or extraordinary acquirement, and, *even then*, it can only be by the prevailing suffrage of society; therefore do not attempt to claim

the acquaintance of those above you, lest you meet a mortifying repulse. Many will say, 'We are just as good as they are, and as respectable'. SO YOU ARE, but yet not fit companions for each other. Society is divided into various orders, each class having its own views, its peculiar education, habits, and tastes; so that the conversation of the one would probably be most uninteresting to the other. It is the fashion to talk of the spread of education and, so far as merely reading and writing go, it is true; but they are only the *first steps* to a cultivated mind, and the literary acquirement of a man of business is necessarily confined to reading the newspaper. *He has no time for any thing else*; and however skilful in his trade, cannot form an idea of that *man's mind* who has devoted all his energies to science or literature. Nay, can you suppose that even the merchant of Portland Place and the occupant of the back parlour to a butcher's shop think and feel alike? Certainly not; and recollect also, that however highly *you may estimate yourself*, the *world* will rather judge you by any other standard than your own.

The English are the most aristocratic democrats in the world; always endeavouring to squeeze through the **the portals of rank and fashion** portals of rank and fashion, and then slamming the door in the face of any unfortunate devil who may happen to be behind them.

Visiting

If you are thrown amongst fashionable people, you must not pay a visit to a lady before two o'clock P.M., nor after four, as, if you call *before* that time, you will interrupt those avocations which more or less occupy *every lady* in the early part of the day: if *later* than four o'clock, you will prevent her driving out.

On returning visits, a card left at the house is generally considered all that is necessary; but, if you are admitted, do not make a morning visit too long, lest you interfere with the engagements of the mistress of the house.

* Never leave your hat in the hall when you pay a morning visit, it makes you look *too much at home*; take it with you into the room.

It was formerly the custom to turn down the corner of a card if your visits were intended for more than one person in a family, and it is even now occasionally done; but it is much better to leave a card for each division – that is, one for the master of the house; another for the mistress; and one for the young ladies. An old lady, desirous of complying with the fashion, of the reason of which she  was ignorant, when calling on a *single lady*, turned down all the four corners!

In society, verbal invitations are often given to balls or concerts, by persons with whom you are only slightly acquainted, and have not previously visited: in such a case, it is proper to leave a card beforehand on the lady at whose house the soirée is to take place; that she may be made acquainted with your name and intention – so that you may be expected; as you may have received an invitation from her husband of which she was ignorant, and he may not be there to present you. Should it so occur, a card previously left will prevent either party looking foolish, or the stranger appearing 'de trop'.

Some doubts having arisen, after a death, as to the proper period of returning cards of 'thanks', for visits of condolence, we believe there to be no fixed time; for, as cards of thanks imply that the bereaved parties are prepared to receive visitors, it must be, with them, *entirely a matter feeling*.

* Do not take upon yourself to do the honours in another man's house, or constitute yourself master of the ceremonies, as you will thereby offend the host and hostess.

* Be careful in company how you defend your friends, unless the conversation be addressed to yourself. Remember that nobody is perfect, and people may sometimes speak the truth; and that, if contradicted, they

people may sometimes speak the truth

are desirous of justifying themselves, and will *prove* what might otherwise have been a matter of doubt.

Tattling

It has somewhere been observed that, 'In good society, a tacit understanding exists that whatsoever conversation may take place shall be to a certain degree sacred, and may not honourably be carried out of it, and repeated to the prejudice of the utterer'. This axiom cannot be too strongly inculcated; as, if such practices were allowed, all confidence would be destroyed, and there would be no end to the mischief caused by silly or malignant people.

Conversations ever have taken place, and ever will, in which opinions are given, and motives scrutinised, truly and justly too, and with decided advantage to the world, as it is oftentimes the only way in which one half of mankind can be put upon their guard against the other; nevertheless, but few people would be pleased to learn that their designs, their foibles, or their weaknesses, had been made the subject of discussion, as most men flatter themselves the world will take them at whatever value they

mischief caused by silly or malignant people

may choose to set upon themselves.

There are none, therefore, so despicable, as those traitors to society who hurry from house to house, laden with the remarks made by one party upon the other; stirring up discord and strengthening hatred wheresoever they appear by whom every unguarded expression is distorted or magnified, and who take a malicious pleasure (too often under the guise of affection) in wounding one friend at the expense of another. This is the bane of country society, and falls particularly heavy on those 'accustomed to all the freedom of thought and frankness of expression of a great capital, and who find it difficult, if not impossible, to adopt the caution so necessary in a small community'. *

* Life of Mackintosh

Consequently, give *your own opinion* of people if you choose, but you are not at liberty to repeat that of others. Only fancy the result of one lady saying to another, 'Well, Maria, what do you think Miss Macaw says of YOU? She says, that you have the thickest ankles, and the thinnest arms, of any girl in the county; with a figure like an *Alligator*, and a head like a *Bison*!!!'

Be cautious how you indulge in *badinage* in the presence of dull, common-place people; they will either get out of temper in consequence of taking what you say literally, or else will stare and wonder at you for being such a ' strange man'. ' Poor Susan!' said a gentleman to a pretty girl. 'Poor, indeed!' replied the lady, with an indignant toss of the head; ' not so poor as *that* comes to. Papa can give us something.' What an anticipation for the sensitive aspirant!

Wit elicits wit; and when such brilliant materials meet, they form the flint and steel of conversation: appreciation is the tinder, which, though not bright in itself, receives and cherishes the scintillations as they fall. Who has not felt his intellect expand with the assurance of having what he says understood? Appreciation certainly *is a talent*.

Never 'talk *at* people' – it is in the worst possible taste, as it is taking an unfair advantage of them: if there be any thing you dislike '*out with it boldly*', and give them an opportunity of explaining, or of defending them-selves – or else *be silent*.

* Do not say a person is 'affable' unless he or she be of very high rank, as it implies condescension. ROYAL *personages* are ' gracious'.

* Do not repeat the name of the person to whom you are speaking, as – 'Indeed, Mr. Stubbs, you don't say so, Sir,' – or, 'Really, Mrs. Fidkins, I quite agree with you, Mrs. Fidkins.' It is a sufficiently bad habit in an equal, but in one of lower rank it becomes an impertinence.

Above all things, do not mistake stiffness for dignity; the very spirit of good breeding consists in being easy and natural yourself – and in

Etiquette is only the *armour* of society

the endeavour to make others the same. Etiquette is only the *armour* of society; and when your position is fairly established, it may be thrown aside, at least so far as is consistent with good feeling and decorum.

Remember that all your guests are equal for the time being, and have a similar claim to your courtesies: nay, if there be a difference shown, those of the lesser rank require a *little more attention* than the rest, that they may not be made to *feel* their inferiority.

Be careful to offer a favour in such a manner as not to offend the delicacy of those whom you wish to serve. Favours may be so conferred as to become insults – if kindness and a desire to oblige induce you to offer an 'attention', do not *press* it after it has been once refused, and so affront ill-tempered or testy people. A friend who had been dining a short distance from London, when about to return, said to one of the party, 'Sir, my carriage is at the door; if agreeable, I shall be happy to take you to town'. 'I am much obliged to you', replied the ungracious Mr. Tubbs, drawing himself up, 'but – *I have a carriage of my own*'.

* Do not cross a room in an anxious manner, and force your way up to a lady merely to receive a bow, as by so doing you attract the eyes of the company towards her. If you are desirous of being noticed by any one in particular, put yourself in their way as if by accident, and do not let them *see* that you have sought them out; unless, indeed, there be something very important to communicate.

Avoid a loud tone of voice in conversation, or a 'horse laugh': both are exceedingly vulgar; and if practised, strangers may think that you have been 'cad' to an omnibus. There is a slightly subdued *patrician tone of voice*, which we fear can only be acquired in good society. Be cautious also how you take the lead in conversation, unless it be forced upon you, lest people reiterate the remark made on a certain occasion upon that '*Brummagem*' Johnson, Doctor Parr – that 'he was like a *great toe* in society; *the most ignoble part of the body, yet ever thrust foremost*'.

There are but few things display worse taste than the introduction of professional topics in general conversation, especially if there be ladies present: men's minds must be miserably ill-stored, who cannot find other subjects for conversation than their own professions. Who has not felt this on having been compelled to listen to clerical 'slang', musty college jokes, and anecdotes divested of all interest beyond the atmosphere of an university; or 'law' jokes, with 'good stories' of 'learned counsel'; *'long yarns'*; or the equally tiresome muster-roll of 'our regiment' – colonels *dead*, maimed majors retired on pensions, subs lost or 'exchanged', gravitating between Boulogne and the King's Bench? – all such exclusive topics being signs either of a limited intellect, or the most lamentable ignorance.

An exceedingly vulgar custom prevails in the northern part of England – that of females using the titles of their husbands as marks of distinction to themselves; as being spoken of, or written to, and even having printed on their cards, 'Mrs. Capt. Gubbins', 'Mrs. Dr. Borax', or the more balmy and euphonious appellation of 'Mrs. Col. Figgins' (generally the flaxen-haired owner of a bilious Colonel, from 'Choultry Plains', and late of Cheltenham). It springs from a desire to show the world how much they are exalted by their husbands' rank above the 'Muggs' and 'Jenkinses' of low life. How oddly 'Mrs. *Alderman* Tibbs', or 'Mrs. *Churchwarden* Hobbs', would sound! To such an extent is this desire for *title* carried, that at Aberdeen a row **The proper mode of distinguishing the wives** of dramp shops near the Pier is placarded as being kept 'Mrs. *Captain* Gordon', 'Mrs. *Captain* M'Dougal', etc., being the consorts of the 'masters' of the trading smacks. The proper mode of distinguishing the wives of various members of the same family is by using the *Christian* name; as Mrs. Edward, Mrs. James, etc., as the case may be.

Never use the term '*genteel*'. Do not speak of '*genteel people*'; it is a low estimate of good breeding, used only by vulgar persons, and from *their* lips implies that union of finery, flippancy, and affectation often found in those but one remove from 'hewers of wood and drawers of water'. Substitute *'well-bred person'*, *'manners of a gentlewoman'*, or of *'a gentleman'*, instead.

There is a shallow attempt at 'fallen greatness', sometimes practised by persons who wish it to be supposed they are below their proper sphere – that of bestowing high-sounding titles upon very ordinary objects; as calling a hackney coach 'the carriage'; or speaking of a gig, or wretched pony chaise, as 'our carriage'; or of a miserable passage, three feet wide, as the 'hall'. This is very foolish, and does not impose upon any one.

Never use the initial of a person's name to designate him; as 'Mr. P.', 'Mrs. C.', 'Miss W.', etc. Nothing is more abominable than to hear a woman speak of her husband as 'Mr. B.'

In speaking to ladies of title, do not say 'my lady', it being only proper for servants and tradespeople so to do; you may occasionally say 'your ladyship', as it shows that you are aware of their claim to the distinction.

Do not offer a person the chair from which you have just risen, unless there be no other in the room.

sure sign of a coarse and ordinary mind

Do not beat the 'devil's tattoo', by drumming with your fingers on a table; it cannot fail to annoy every one within hearing, and is the index of a vacant mind. Neither read the newspaper in an audible whisper, as it disturbs the attention of those near you. Both these bad habits are particularly offensive where most common; that is, in a country news-room. Remember, that a carelessness as to what may incommode others is the sure sign of a coarse and ordinary mind; indeed, the essential part of good breeding is more in the avoidance of whatever may be disagreeable to others, than even an accurate observance of the customs of good society.

Never allow any person above the rank of a shopman to leave the room without your ringing the bell for the street door to be opened. Thousands have been irremediably offended by having been suffered to quit a room unattended, and to 'let themselves out'. This deserves particular notice, as it is a very common omission with persons, who, having amassed a little wealth and set up for *somebodies*, would be exceedingly annoyed to have it whispered that they could be guilty of such gross ill breeding.

People who have risen in the world are too apt to suppose they render themselves of consequence *in proportion to the pride they display*, and their want of attention towards those with whom they come in contact: this is a terrible mistake, as every ill-bred act recoils with triple violence against its perpetrators, by leading the offended parties to analyse them, and to question the right of assuming a superiority to which (in the absence of *positive rank*) they are but rarely entitled.

The fear of being thought vulgar often drives meritorious people, who have risen by their own exertions, into the opposite extreme, and causes them to be superlatively delicate. Such persons are shocked at the sound of '*breeches*', will substitute 'inebriated' for '*very drunk*', and cannot be brought to allow there are such animals as '*women*' in the world.

It is also a clumsy attempt at refinement to use a particular *set* of words: at present we have '*splendid* travelling', '*splendid* gin', '*splendid* potatoes', etc.

Do not abuse the advantage of a ' twopenny post', by making people pay the postage of letters on *your own* business merely, and transmitted through such a channel entirely for *your convenience*, by saving the trouble of sending a servant. The postage upon one solitary note is small, it is true; but may have risen by amount to a large sum in the aggregate. Depend upon it, the most '*tiffy*' people will not be very much offended at the postage being paid, although some affect *openly* to despise an expense at which they grumble in *secret*.

With intimate friends, you may dispense with ceremony as much as may be deemed desirable to all parties; but with strangers, or persons with whom you are only imperfectly acquainted, every deviation from established custom *is a slight*, as it tends to show how little their society is appreciated; and will (if they possess a grain of spirit) be resented accordingly.

Although these remarks will not be sufficient in themselves to *make* you a *gentleman*, yet they will enable you to avoid any glaring impropriety, and do much to render you easy and confident in society.

Gentility is neither in birth, manner, nor fashion – but in *the* MIND. A high sense of honour – a determination never to take a mean advantage of another – an adherence to truth, delicacy, and politeness towards those with whom you may have dealings – are the essential and distinguishing characteristics of a GENTLEMAN.

THE END

Other titles from Summersdale

ESSENTIAL
BEETON

Recipes and tips from the original domestic goddess

ISABELLA BEETON

Essential Beeton
Recipes and Tips from
the Original Domestic Goddess
Isabella Beeton
£9.99 Hb

The indefatigable Isabella Beeton was crowned the domestic goddess long before Nigella started licking chocolate off her fingers. Encapsulating the cream of her *Book of Household Management*, the most famous English cookery book ever published, *Essential Beeton* includes pearls of wisdom on housework (and the importance of elbow grease), home hairdressing, a cure for the common cold and, of course, some of Mrs B's most celebrated recipes.

Pot-Pourri From a Surrey Garden

THE CLASSIC DIARY OF A VICTORIAN LADY

MRS C. W. EARLE

Pot-Pourri From a Surrey Garden
The Classic Diary of a Victorian Lady
Mrs C. W. Earle
£9.99 Hb

First published in 1897, *Pot-Pourri from a Surrey Garden* was widely acclaimed by Mrs Earle's Victorian readership as the book that made gardening and naturalism fashionable.

Mrs Earle spent the winter months in London and the rest of the year in Surrey where her beloved garden took up most of her time.

She claimed she was not going to write 'a gardening book, or a cookery book, or a book on furnishing or education' – and yet *Pot-Pourri from a Surrey Garden* is all of these.

Written in the form of a diary, and with a refreshing frankness and charm that will delight modern readers, Mrs Earle intersperses her astute observations with recipes and gardening tips in a book that embodies a passion for country life – as fascinating and useful now as it was over 100 years ago.

TEA

A DRINK WITH
JAM AND BREAD

VICKY EDWARDS

Tea, a Drink with Jam and Bread
Vicky Edwards
£4.99 Hb

In China many moons ago a thirsty emperor and a happy accident introduced what was to become the world's most famous drink. This perfectly brewed book is a delightful blend of teatime etiquette, history, recipes, Britain's finest tea shops and bags more besides.

Vicky Edwards invites you to raise a bone china cup and a well-cocked finger to celebrate this liquid refreshment with leaf lovers everywhere.

What the Victorians
didn't do for us

A collection of their useless advice

ALASTAIR WILLIAMS

What the Victorians Didn't Do For Us
A Collection of Their Useless Advice
Alastair Williams
£7.99 Hb

The Victorians may have given us the Industrial
Revolution and advances in medicine and science,
but they also relied on child labour and extolled
the benefits of opium.

This book features advice from the lesser of the
nineteenth century agony aunts.

Did you know that washing your teeth with
charcoal was once believed to make them whiter?
That ladies were encouraged to drink vinegar to
appear pale and delicate?

From the strange to the downright unsavoury,
learn what the Victorians didn't do for us.

www.summersdale.com